What others are

"A delightful book.... It just kept me smiling."

Ken Stein
Political Commentator/ Little League Coach

"$\frac{(\text{tears} + \text{smiles}^2)}{\text{friends}} = \text{Frankly Speaking}$"

Anne Creden
Bartender/Physics Teacher

"It really made me laugh. I think it would be neat to give to my kids someday."

Andrew
10 Year Old

"*Frankly Speaking* is just that...the entertaining and insightful mumblings of a world class analogist.
Savor these tidbits of wisdom."

Tom Korchak
Product Manager, W.R. Grace & Co.

"Lots of good food for thought served in a very digestible manner."

Glen Gurevitch
Restaurateur

"*Frankly Speaking*'s blend of philosophy and humor will touch you...and it won't let you go."

Laurie Donnelly
Miss Fitness America

"No comment."

The White House

FRANKLY SPEAKING

By J. Frank Shaffer

Gunter Publishing, Atlanta, Georgia

Published by:
Gunter Publishing
2870 Peachtree Road
Suite 133
Atlanta, GA 30305

Publisher's Cataloging in Publication Data
Shaffer, J. Frank / Frankly Speaking
I. Title
Library of Congress Catalog Card Number: 94-76871

ISBN 0-9641852-8-8

Printed in the United States of America
Book design by Diva Designs
For further information or to order copies,
please call 404-233-9148 or 800-989-1133,
or write to Gunter Publishing.

Author's Note:

People would frequently tell me "you should write that down." Many times "that" would grow once written down. Many passages that are only a few sentences could have easily been ten or twenty pages long. However, this brevity will hopefully serve as a doorway to the reader's own experiences. Please read at your own speed. After all, only you can read at "your own pace." I sincerely hope you enjoy the book.

Acknowledgements:

Many of the people who helped to make this book possible are mentioned directly or indirectly in its pages:

— Thanks for your editing help; Graham, Leo, and Tom.

— Thank you to everyone who so generously lent me their ears. Many people's contributions are acknowledged in the book either directly or indirectly.

— To V.J., Bruce, and Bob; they say "You're never too old to have a happy childhood." Thanks to you all and Naaman's Gardens, I already have.

— Thanks, Mom, for your generous ears and heart.

— And to Terry, thanks for your help with the cartoons and the unselfish example you have always set for me.

— As for Tracy and Roger, you all get your just rewards in the book.

— The following have also made specific contributions;

Martha and Pete Gilley, the Korchak family, the Scollard family, Russ Broda, Terry O'Donohue, Lisa and Lib Morgan, the Israel family, Nancy Prittie, and Michelle Gillen.

—To the next generation; Jessica, Nicole, and Alexandra McAlvany, and Nicole Korchak — beware of Austins bearing gifts.

—To all my AFS families; especially the Ozdemirs, the Walters, the Everinghams, the Oakleys, and the Negretes.

— And of course, all my other family, friends, and teammates. To all the above, I am truly grateful.

There are no dedications at the beginning of this book — they're all inside.

Table of Contents

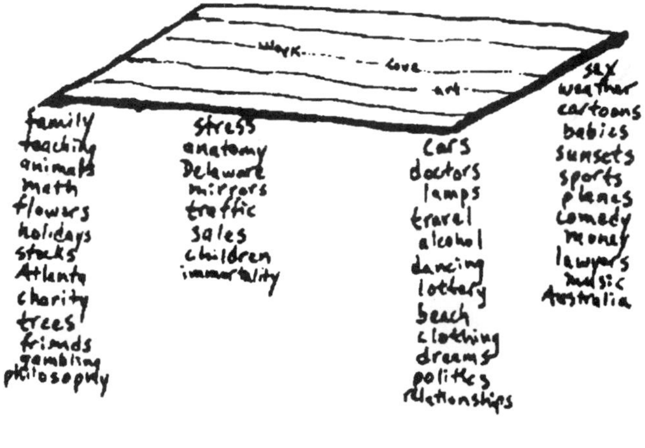

-1-

I think *everyone* who makes generalizations is wrong.

◆

The mind is a muscle that needs to be exercised like any other. Otherwise, you are left with Rolf Mueller—an unknown German with a great throwing arm who never picked up a baseball.

◆

A smile is a brilliant cover letter for your resume.

◆

It's interesting how upon first meeting someone usually the first question is, "So, what do you do?" Everyone interprets this as what you do "for a living". Usually when it comes to "living", most people do things more interesting than their "job".

However, the unfortunate byproduct of this first question is how it immediately biases us in our opinions of another. If the person to your right on a plane is a toll booth operator and the person on your left a chemical engineer — are your conceptions of these people vastly different after just one question? Isn't this discrimination? Does a blind person ask if you are white or black? Let's come up with a better line of questioning in our initial interview, i.e., — So, have you read any good books lately?

◆

Sometimes when I leave a room, I just throw a piece of paper in the middle of the floor. This is called a "mnemonic device" — it helps me remember to do something when I return. This works better for me than tying a string around my finger. I'd much rather be thought of as "sloppy" than having a memory problem.

◆

The more diversity used in one's search — the less narrow-minded their answer will be.

◆

Ideas aren't necessarily particular to individual people. There are over four billion inhabitants in the world — so probably somebody, somewhere, has had the same thought as you.

There were many who hoped to be the first to fly across the Atlantic Ocean. But, Charles Lindbergh is the one who did it. It is not the dream that separates us, but rather the subsequent action upon it.

—◆—◆—

-2-

You know what they say, if it ain't broken, take it to an automotive shop and they'll fix it.

◆

To most people I'm a quiet person. "He's a quiet guy, never said a lot, kinda kept to himself."

Much like the Porsche and Honda which are equally quiet in shyness and performance when the engine is off. However, turn on the ignition, and in one case you're carrying babies around and in the other one you're making them. In my case, I drive a '68 Plymouth Satellite convertible in need of paint.

◆

If everyone took their foot off the brake pedal at the same time when a light turned green — would we have any traffic?

◆

New bumper sticker: "If you can read this — I'd rather be driving faster."

◆

Isn't almost everything we do in life "gambling"?

Just getting into a car is a bit of a risk isn't it? How about picking which line to get into while at the grocery store? How many of us have a winning record at this casino? I also gamble on the left lane when driving. Your reward is an unencumbered breeze through traffic — all the while there is the peril of a "left turner" who neglects to use their blinker. I've lost my shirt gambling on that left lane — I still can't resist sometimes.

Anyway, I hope they don't ever bring casinos to Atlanta. Just getting in a car and driving in the left lane to the grocery store is about all I can handle.

◆

Next time you ask someone for directions, ask them how you get here from there. Write it down. Then hold the directions up to the mirror.

◆

When you borrow a car — return it with a full tank of gas. The idea is to have people lining up to lend you things.

◆

Don't you just love those "Men Working" signs on the road? I'm sorry, but maybe I'm one of those people who don't believe everything I read. Shouldn't they change the sign to "Men Standing Around Causing Traffic"? If they were really working, would they have time to put up a sign to remind themselves?

—◆—◆—

-3-

Remember, everybody is exactly like no one else.

◆

A percentage of profits from this book will go to charity. Some companies already donate a percentage of sales to charity. They usually don't start doing this until they're already making millions — that's okay — better late than never like most companies. I will donate starting with my first dollar. If this helps sales, is it wrong to profit further in the name of charity? Is it right not to?

◆

It seems like most of the genuinely kind people in the world don't even realize it. That may be what puts them at the top of their class.

◆

Aren't the world's problems just like mowing the lawn? Every second of every day, somebody is mowing a lawn somewhere. Thing is, you never hear it until it's close to you and then the noise can be very disturbing. How often do people wait until something happens to them or their loved ones until they get involved. Volunteer for a landscaping company today — the next lawn you save may be your own!

—◆—◆—

-4-

"Possession is nine-tenths of the law." Legal fees eat up the other half.

◆

There is a reason I use so many people's actual names in this book. It is a great way to endear them to you and gain their support. However, under advice of my attorney, Williame Dexvprymutpy, I have been instructed to spell their names wrong just in case.

◆

Many people think the law should fully compensate us for our losses. Usually it can only mitigate our damages.

◆

Why is it when you give some people a baseball uniform they think they're a baseball player, or give them a stethoscope and they think they're a doctor? Just be whatever you are and not an expert on everything all the time. I know this to be true — I'm an expert in this field.

◆

Successful surgery always starts with fear and pain.

◆

Which came first, the chicken or the egg?

It doesn't really matter — the lawyers will get paid before either of them prove their case.

—◆—◆—

-6-

Philosophy is everything with more than one answer.

◆

Have you ever heard the saying, "It's not what you do, but how you do it." Well, I think we could probably add to that, "It's not what you do, but the sequence in which you do it." Can you imagine always showering before jogging, or never having room for the main course after eating dessert? What a smelly malnourished country we would become. Should we change the dating process to kissing, coffee, and then a movie — then how many dates would get past the 1st inning? Yes, the world is full of sequence, without which there would probably be total anarchy.

And sure, most of the sequence makes sense absolute and good this is. However, if you don't ever try putting the number 6 right after the number 4, you probably won't ever truly appreciate the number 5.

◆

Facts are but an echo — questions inspire.

◆

It's interesting how vaccines work. They actually cure you by giving you a taste of what's bad. Yes, that's right, the vaccine injection actually contains some of the disease and that works to prevent you from getting sick. Maybe everyone should spend a day in a slum before we can truly attack poverty.

◆

Why did you like or dislike the last one on page 18?

◆

Yes, I still have some shirts with a crocodile or some kind of reptile on it. These were quite popular 10 years ago but maybe the wildlife committee thought it cruel because I don't see so many anymore. I also have some shirts with a guy on a horse. These seem quite popular and have flourished in a variety of habitats. I also have one shirt with a guy falling off his horse. Of course, this is my favorite shirt although apparently the embarrassment of such an event has made it difficult to find such shirts.

I wondered about the differences between all these shirts. They were all short sleeved and made of cotton — only the picture over the heart was different. I know I won't ever be able to make people judge one another by what's inside the shirt rather than the outside. So in the meantime, I may start a designer shirt collection with someone sliding into home.

A percentage of profits will go to charity. There will also be a 20% discount to proven baseball fans. Then, perhaps, for the first time we may actually see into someone's heart rather than their pocket.

◆

Sometimes when I'm alone with my thoughts — I can't get a word in edgewise.

◆

Sometimes life is like holding a mirror up to a mirror. When it comes to your successes — hold up the mirror — as for your mistakes, drop the mirror before the mistakes are compounded.

—◆—◆—

-7-

Aren't books like oreo cookies? Should just a few people have decided whether an oreo tasted good? Books are like food in that ultimately only the public can make the final decision. So, enjoy your meal and watch out for the anchovies.

◆

To Graham: my buddy at CNN who writes for Headline News. Now I know how you feel at the end of a workday — this writing stuff is tough. For me, that brain muscle is just out of shape. Kinda like jogging for the first time in years. I just hope my face doesn't look like a jogger's when I write.

◆

This paragraph is dedicated to all the good analogies that came into my head only to vanish shortly thereafter without the chance of preservation. I enjoyed thinking of you for an instant and may you touch others someday in some way. Say hi to Amelia Earhart for me.

◆

After reading various parts of this book to friends, I soon realized my relentless nature in this regard might cause them to hang up on me, or just altogether quit talking to me. I did not want this to happen and I knew friends might not be totally objective in their remarks.

Consequently, I embarked on my own marketing research campaign — I cold called people out of the phone book! I knew people got cold-called all the time, but never before from an aspiring author eager to try his goods on an unsuspecting public. I called up Archie Lowe of Atlanta and said, "Hi, my name is Frank Shaffer and I'm writing a book of analogies and wondered if I might read some to you. I randomly picked your name out of the phone book and feel that you as a total stranger would be able to give me totally objective feelings about my work — after all, you as the general public will be my ultimate editor anyway."

I was appreciative of all the cooperation I received and I think the public liked the idea of a sales pitch without anything to sell. I really enjoyed the whole experiment and look forward to meeting some of my victims one day. Some responses were positive and some were negative. But you know what they say, "You can't fool all of the people all of the time, but you can fool some of the people some of the time." — I just want to fool a million people one time while they're in a book store.

-8-

Can you imagine if intellect were something you could stare at in a shopping mall and looks were something that required a concerted effort to get to know?

I initially thought this scenario might help my romance situation. However, upon further consideration, I soon realized in either case I'd probably end up drinking alone at the bar.

◆

Do unto others as you would have...I frequently wave at women.

◆

Is "don't you think all pick-up lines are stupid" a good pick-up line?

◆

Wouldn't it be neat if we could control our dreams. Imagine going to bed at night and deciding, "I'm going to have a wet dream." Problem is, before you know it, instead of taking lunch breaks everybody would be taking power naps and retiring early after dinner.

P.S. — This would add a whole new trauma to sleeping disorders.

— Masters & Johnson would have to come out with a book on them.

— The number of insomniacs would either quadruple or disappear, I'm not sure which.

— Guys would hang out and brag about how long their naps are and how many they're capable of in a day.

— Women would say how "He thought I was asleep but I was really faking it."

— . . . .

◆

What is the difference between a good pool shot and a great pool shot? In a good pool shot there are several trajectories that will work, while in a great pool shot there is precisely one trajectory that will work. Isn't that what defines perfection — hitting something on that one trajectory line with no margin of error?

In life, there are plenty of good women out there, but I haven't found my perfect shot yet — I guess I need to get working on my pool game.

◆

When it comes to dating — "Most men lead lives of quiet desperation." The rest of us are just more vocal about it.

◆

Good looks may or may not help a poor personality — but kindness will always make someone beautiful.

—◆—◆—

-9-

Tons of people "make it" by working hard. I just wanted to make sure I had exhausted the possibility of not having to work hard, before I started working hard. The first possibility has always been my dream. Please help my dream come true and buy this book.

◆

Sometimes it is better to strike out swinging than to walk.

◆

As part of my ongoing research campaign, I felt obligated to take my work to the public in many different methods. With this in mind, I entered the real world jungle of the Atlanta bar and restaurant scene. I randomly selected beautiful women to read samples and give me their thoughts. Being of sound scientific mind, I realized this study group was perhaps slanted, yet I persisted. Why was I able to approach women I would have otherwise let disappear into the night?

I knew meeting women was a difficult sales job — especially in my case. As a salesman you're usually only allowed one or two sentences and most times you have no appointment, so it's especially difficult to gain office access. Why was I being so much more bold in my sales campaign?

As with most sales, when you truly believe in your product — it comes across to your prospective client. I've never been much of a salesman, but I know if I truly believe in something — it's no longer sales.

◆

Money is made from paper — paper is made from wood — money grows on trees.

◆

Sometimes I'd rather be in the market for computer paper than a jet. I know computer paper isn't as glamorous as jets, but it does have its advantages. In both cases, the salesman will treat you well on the first meeting and subsequent sale. However, this is where the paths change direction. The jet salesman is now ready to move on to his next potential bounty. You hold no more commissionable appeal to him.

Meanwhile, the computer paper guy will come back to service your account as often as needed — a relationship has formed.

The goal in life, as in business, is to wake up Monday morning with as many relationships as the market will bear.

P.S. — That's not to say a jet also in need of computer paper wouldn't be a good sale.

◆

Ah — Philosophy/Writer. Now there's a job someone can do comfortably while sitting on the beach without seeming like a wanker by having a phone next to them at all times.

◆

Sometimes the work place is kinda like a grocery store line. The "higher ups" may tend to think they are above everyone, but maybe they just got in line before us. Eventually we will all be at home having paid the same price for milk.

◆

If you can find a job where you like your work — you won't have to for a living.

◆

Do those subscription cards that fall out of magazines really bug you? If we are already looking at the magazine — is it likely we would need another copy? Do they really think making us pick this card up off the floor will inspire us to buy? Do the successful salesmen in the world make us lift something to close the sale?

"I really think you'll like this heavy winter coat Mrs. Attfield. Go ahead, pick it up off the floor a couple of times and see if you like it."

—◆—◆—

-10-

If you listen to the same radio station all the time — you'll only hear one type of song.

◆

Direct your own movie and you'll always have a part.

◆

They said on TV today that George Brett is announcing his retirement tomorrow. Didn't this story just announce his retirement? Maybe part of the announcement tomorrow will be that the announcement made today is still correct.

◆

If you're always busy listening to your own song — you'll never hear any of Beethoven's music.

◆

Let's start an art museum experiment with Claude Monet, Jean KMart, and Rolf Volkswagen paintings in it. All the KMart and Volkswagen paintings aren't famous, but are very similar in style to Monet. We will take all the people from section 115 at the Braves Stadium and have them come to the museum and rank their favorite paintings. The next day we'll do it all over again except we'll switch the names on the paintings. Would Monet win almost all the time?

◆

Until you come and look at the view out my window, you'll never fully understand my painting.

—◆—◆—

-11-

I've never learned from a mistake I didn't admit to.

◆

clandestine (klan-des-tin) — adjective meaning "kept secret".

Did some guys named Oxford and Webster hang out and discuss this word before putting it in the dictionary?

"Hey Web, what does the word clandestine mean?"

"Well, Ox, I'm not really sure, no one will give me a straight answer."

"Wow, it must be some important government word cuz everyone I talked to says it's definition is kept secret."

"What do you think we should do Web?"

"Why don't we just put down it's *kept secret* until the government declassifies the word and makes public the real meaning."

◆

You know what they say, "If you can't do it well, it ain't worth doing." — This might explain why I have so much time on my hands.

◆

Always judge a page by its content — not the quantity of its content.

◆

Math 101

12	x	dishonesty	=	0
(family + friends)	x	1	=	happiness
1	+	1	=	love
2	÷	divorce	=	2 – 1
3	÷	divorce	=	parent – child
2	+	child	=	1,000,000
Newborn	x	1	=	1,000,000 – sleep
Everything	+	1	=	Family

◆

~~I've written lots of papers in my time.~~
~~They usually all had an introduction, body, and conclusion.~~

If a conclusion is strong enough, it shouldn't need an introduction or explanation.

◆

The more I learn, the more I know about the past and the more confident I am about things I could never know concerning the future.

◆

Why do people do so well in some subjects and so poorly in others? Einstein failed math didn't he? I wish the SAT's had a score for analogies. I got over 700 on my math SAT's but did much poorer on the verbal section — I guess I should have known then I could never be a writer.

◆

That which is learned from a mistake, is often the seed to success.

◆

The three most important rules to editing are: 1) Be brief.

◆

You may be wondering — does he actually heed all the stuff he writes about — not even close. Life is one of those tests scored on a bell curve where no one gets a 100%. It helps some of us to learn by seeing things written down. Some of us learn by writing ourselves, or teaching. Unfortunately in life, too many people are content with barely passing. I know I probably won't finish at the top of my class — but that doesn't mean I'll ever quit studying.

◆

Shouldn't all tests be open book on more material than we could ever memorize — Isn't that what life is?

—◆—◆—

-12-

If beauty is in the eyes of the beholder — perhaps more people need contact lenses.

◆

Confidence is knowing you are correct or capable of doing something well — declaring this information is usually just bragging.

◆

Lots of things in life fall under the "8 X 0" theory. What is the "8 X 0" theory you ask? If somebody doesn't know anything, and they get 8 times smarter — are they any smarter?

I could have written seven more examples of the "8 X 0" theory. However, if you didn't like the first one, and I wrote seven more, would you like the first one any better?

◆

I'd rather have 20-40 foresight than 20-20 hindsight.

◆

I have a reputation for being late. This is not a particularly good reputation to have. I'm not quite sure how it developed as usually I was on time; however, there were also many times I was late.

Why did I have this reputation and my friend Martha did not? Certainly she had been late before. Martha also had a reputation for being a nice person. Had she acquired this reputation through one thing she had done 10 years ago? No — she was kind day in and day out — *repetition develops reputations*. Finally, I had figured out how to develop a good reputation. It took me a while, and as usual I was late — but hopefully I will arrive at my destination.

P.S. — I wrote this on my way to a meeting — causing me to be late.

—◆—◆—

-13-

Do unto others as you would have them do unto you or your mother.

◆

Aren't the clouds like parents? I was on a jet last weekend and noticed once we got above the clouds there was nothing but sunshine. Were those stupid clouds below doing the world a great injustice by blocking all this beautiful sunshine?

No, in scientific truth, the clouds and atmosphere act as a filter to protect us from damaging ultraviolet rays.

So, next time a parent seems to be raining on our parade — they may just be a protective cloud hoping to bring us more sunshine in the future.

◆

To: Terry,

Thanks for all those pepper games in the backyard. You have been a good mentor for the word "brother".

◆

The pictures on the following page are a get well card I sent a childhood friend. He had experienced a difficult year as his father had passed away and four months later he was in the hospital getting his stomach operated on.

We have known each other forever and climbed lots of trees as kids. Consequently, I came up with the idea of a get well card consisting of several photos of me climbing a tree. The last photo was a zoom-up of me holding a piece of cardboard saying "Get Well." He said he cried when he saw the last picture.

Anyway, he has come a long way since then. Bruce — keep up the good work and remember, no one ever got a "Comeback Player of the Year" award without first having a rough season.

P.S. — Yes, I did write this while revisiting the top of the tree. It's getting dark now — I better climb down.

No one has ever climbed to the top of a tree without the kindness of many branches.

◆

To everyone whose father has passed away:

I remember when my father passed away, it was the saddest period of my whole life. He was 61 years old and truly a brilliant person in every capacity. I remember thinking how access to all his accumulated experiences, knowledge, and wisdom had just been turned off — the library was suddenly closed.

Really what happened was the library just moved to another neighborhood. Someday I'll move up to that neighborhood, and the first thing I'll do is renew my library card.

—◆—◆—

-14-

I bet if there was another profession that critiqued critic's criticisms — the critics wouldn't be so critical.

◆

I'm great at being modest.

◆

It's not so important to worry or not about what other people think as it is to be comfortable with whatever level you choose.

◆

If you think you built it — they will come.

◆

If you've never peaked before — is it possible to peak too soon?

◆

Critics' Comments

"It's a triple — he never had the power to yank one out."

Jon Frank Shaffer
Softball Player

"It's funny, compelling, and stupid — all in one syllable."

J. Frank Shaffer
Writer

"If you don't own the book — it's a screaming buy. If you already own the book — our research department says sell. Either way I'll get a commission."

Jon Shaffer
Stockbroker

"I'm not very impressionist with it — way too many words and not enough pictures."

Frankie Shaffer
Painter

"You might say it's a walk, followed by a stolen base, a ground ball to second, and a sacrifice fly. Somehow, he managed to score a run without even getting a hit!"

Frank Shaffer
Braves Fan

"It's a feeling of having traveled around the world and standing exactly where you started. To someone else it may seem like you never left. Yet, the reader knows they have not only traveled around the world, but have also been moved by the experience."

Jon Frank Parsons Shaffer
Philosopher

◆

Everybody is perfect in some ways.

◆

You know what they say —" It is better to remain quiet and seem a fool, than to speak up and remove all doubt." This is one of my favorite sayings. I say it all the time.

—◆—◆—

-15-

I used to be in the camp "that money isn't important". Then I realized, in order to objectively evaluate this statement, I would also need to be rich. I only want to be rich to help me validate my feeling that money isn't important.

◆

There are no opinions in the stock market, only right and wrong as measured by what price you bought and sold at.

◆

In horse racing, one cheers for a horse usually because he or she will benefit financially. In the stock market you root for a stock because it may make you financially secure. As a sports fan, you cheer for a team in the purest sense imaginable, the reason for which I'm not quite sure.

◆

A 50% return on a $10,000 portfolio isn't as good as a 5% return on a million dollar portfolio. The more you save now, the better your returns will be later on.

◆

In baseball we keep score with runs, in sleeping with hours, in basketball with points, and football with touchdowns. In life unfortunately, too many people think we keep score with dollars — but dollars are really only a tool to success like a batting glove in baseball. The real success/wins/runs in life comes from happiness and fulfillment. I'd much rather be on the team with the most wins than the most batting gloves.

◆

Everybody has to "pay their dues" eventually. Some just charge it on their Visa card.

◆

On the issue of "what do I do." All this writing stuff has my professional identity confused. Can I say I'm a writer — but I haven't had anything published. If that happens will I then be able to get a business card with "author" on it? Exactly where is the cut-off between hobby and profession? Do you have to make money at what you do in order to qualify as something? If this were true, Van Gogh would never have been a painter until after he was dead! Is a business card as good after you're dead?

Perhaps you "are" what you're good at and enjoy first, and the rest is just batting gloves.

◆

They say a criminal always returns to the scene of the crime. If that were true, there'd be more prisons getting robbed.

-16-

Spring is always at its best after a long winter.

◆

Aren't Hanukkah and Christmas similar to volleyball? I've never really liked volleyball — I'm short, I've never played it very much, and it's played inside too often. But those are all excuses — fact is, I've never been very good at the game.

As for Christmas and Hanukkah, they're great traditions although I usually thought shopping for X'mas presents was kind of a pain. I never really know what to get anyone, and the malls are packed, and I'm kinda short, and…

Your affinity for things are usually proportionate to your ability to do them well. I may never become much of a volleyball player — but as for Christmas, I'm hoping this December is one of my best seasons.

◆

Holidays are when it feels like Sunday night, but it's actually only Friday.

◆

There is no storm worse than the one you're in.

◆

So many things in life can seem insurmountable. However, much like a baseball player in spring training hoping for a good year — we can't start the season with 35 homers, a gold glove award, and 200 hits. Just be patient and take it one game at a time, and when October rolls around — the stats will be there.

◆

Shopping for oneself will numb today's pain. But giving to others is the elixir of tomorrow.

◆

I'm one of those people who really loves the beach. Strangely enough, I live in Atlanta, a good five hours from the coast. At least I know not to take it for granted when I am fortunate enough to be near the ocean.

While in Costa Rica, I had the wonderful dilemma of trying to decide whether I preferred the Caribbean or the Pacific Ocean. Everything else aside, on the issue of the sun and water, I've always enjoyed sunsets on the ocean more than sunrises. People who know me may suspect that sleeping is prohibitive to sunrise enjoyment; but, there's more to it than that. Certainly they both exalt in terms of beauty; but, they differ in terms of timing. If I knew I was only going to get one game-winning hit, I would prefer it in the ninth inning with a glass of wine.

◆

No one can smile back at you until you have smiled at them.

—◆—◆—

-17-

It's funny how no matter where you go in the world, dogs will chase cars and people will be in a rush to stand up and wait when their plane lands.

◆

While on the way to L.A. airport, the shuttle driver went straight when I clearly saw a sign that said "L.A. Airport turn left here." I was well aware of the town's affinity for traffic, but it still seemed odd to me. Anyway, I just figured "he must know something I don't."

So many people say that line without really believing it. Could a driver actually know something I didn't know? Sure enough, it was a shortcut. Fact is, everybody knows something we don't know. Until we realize this — we'll never know as much as they do.

◆

You can't fully appreciate the view from the top of a mountain until you've been through a valley.

◆

I often think back to my first days out of college when I was an aircraft broker. I remember a very wealthy guy who showed up to look at a jet he was interested in buying. He was wearing cut-offs and a t-shirt while deciding whether to dish out several million dollars for a jet. I wondered about the irony of it all and thought if I ever bought a jet, I would dress the same way. Please help me be ironic and buy my book. Of course if you're reading this you've probably already bought the book, so buy another one for a friend so I can be really ironic.

◆

We've all heard the saying, "It's a nice place to visit, but I wouldn't want to live there." Some of us have lived in places we don't like. Then the saying would probably be, "I've lived there and you wouldn't want to visit."

As for Costa Rica, it's a great place to visit but I'm not sure about finding your way around the towns. The streets aren't marked and the houses don't have any numbers. A typical mailing address for someone would be "north to town of Heredia, left at church for 100 meters, then right, third house on right."

I guess this isn't the most efficient way to deliver mail. Yet somehow if I were a letter being sent into the unknown, I'd feel much more at home around the corner from a church than at Apt. #12, at 147, 15th St.

◆

Sometimes you have to learn to fly before you ever get your wings.

◆

It's funny how when we meet a person from somewhere we used to live — we kinda make a big deal of it.

"Oh really, you used to live in Delaware? So did I. What high school did you go..."

Now that I think about it, I'm not really sure what the big deal is. If we were looking for a "living in the same town coincidence," why wouldn't we just go down the street about a mile?

"Knock, knock"

"Hi, what can I do for you?"

"Well, I live down the street about a mile from here."

"Really, wow — I also live in Atlanta about a mile *up* the street from you..."

◆

It's a small world sometimes — the rest of the time it's on steroids.

—◆—◆—

-18-

If looks can be deceiving, how come all our mothers are so beautiful?

◆

When I first began writing all these, I would read them to friends and family over the phone. I found this a little frustrating since I couldn't see their facial reactions. I couldn't tell whether they were smiling, frowning, or about to cry, because I was only able to use one of my senses — hearing. It made me realize how important all the senses are to communication. Amazingly, the telephone provided me with a glimpse at what it would be like to be blind. Please don't handicap yourself — use all your senses.

◆

I've gotten lots of presents over the years from my brother, but the one I remember most is a lamp he made.

◆

To my brother-in-law Roger, who I used to give abuse about not living in modern society because he had no answering machine. I hope I get to that level of psychological self-sufficiency some day.

◆

They say a sucker is born every minute. My mother must have been in labor for days when she had me.

◆

Tonight I read some of my work to my sister for the first time. I held off doing this for some time as I wanted to make sure I was properly prepared for whom I considered to be an important client. She laughed loudly at some and actually cried on the one regarding our father, all within a matter of moments. She truly is someone in possession of a full library of pure and special emotions.

I saw through this time we had together the true power of communication. Her laughing made me laugh at something I had probably already read ten times. And when she cried — I cried. Having someone that close to you enjoy it so much was like the difference between watching the winner of a lottery on TV, and actually winning the lottery myself.

Yet, I knew there was more to it. There was another

more important lottery I had really won — the million dollar lottery ticket I was holding was my sister named Tracy.

—◆—◆—

-19-

I never met anyone who hit a home run without touching first base.

◆

I play some individual sports like tennis and some team sports like baseball. When it comes to celebrations — I usually enjoyed having people put me on their shoulders more than pouring champagne on myself.

◆

Cardinal knowledge is realizing their baseball team (owned by Anheiser Busch) was founded on "the more you drink, the more $$ we make, the better our team gets."

◆

Eating healthy is like a sacrifice bunt that moves the runner along putting him in a better position to score. When smoking, not only do you fail to move the runner along — you also cause him to get picked off.

◆

Sunsets at the beach make me realize I could never be a good golfer — I like the sand and water way too much.

◆

Being a pitcher who can't throw strikes is like a Sumo wrestler entering the 100M breaststroke — he can still win but it's a lot tougher and it ain't pretty.

◆

Why does society say "he's not an engineer anymore, or she doesn't teach anymore, they're retired." Does a parent quit being a parent once the children have grown up and moved away? I'm sorry, but I will always be a baseball player and fan whether I'm off the field, on the field, or in my dreams.

◆

I've never caught a ball just out of my reach by not diving.

—◆—◆—

-20-

There are two records in baseball I doubt will ever be broken. The first is Hank Aaron's career home run record, and the other is the number of game winning hits in a nine inning contest.

◆

I worked as an usher for the Atlanta Braves in 1991 — what an incredible season. Would you believe I received an employee of the month award in June of that year? I still have the plaque in my room, although they misspelled my last name. There was one other incorrect spelling — "Employee" should have been spelled "Fan".

A painter named Nicholas Mazzone drew this picture of me working the Braves game (his father is the Braves pitching coach.) Thanks for signing your work Nicholas.

◆

To my friend, nine-year-old Andrew Stein, who I took up the Braves tunnel after three pitchers threw a combined no-hitter. The excitement and joy you felt — well, I was right there with you.

◆

Like Crash Davis said in the movie Bull Durham, "It's one hit a week that separates the .250 hitter from a .300 hitter." I've been a .250 hitter for a long time, I'm ready for that next plateau. If we all start running out our ground balls, maybe we can all be .300 hitters. Problem is, if we're all .300 hitters, it's not such a big deal anymore! Fortunately, some people are slow runners like Sid Bream.

So, like Satchel Paige said, don't look back — Sid Bream may be gaining on you.

—◆—◆—

-21-

It's not what you know, but who knows you know it.

◆

It's interesting how different professions have different maturity dates. Child stars at a young age, athletes in their late 20's, male actors in their 30's, yuppies in their 40's, CEOs in their 50's, and Presidents in their 60's. I guess the muscles in some professions atrophy with age while in other professions the muscle being used actually strengthens with age. This might explain why Lenny Dykstra would be a scary President and Bill Clinton looks so goofy when he jogs.

◆

How could we truly appreciate our successes if we never had any failures?

◆

Successful people should always invite those over for dinner who first liked their cooking. At least then they'll know the guest really likes the food and not just the atmosphere.

◆

Success is like a flower — I always enjoyed giving flowers more than buying them for myself.

—◆—◆—

-22-

The "half of the time" it takes to market a book takes longer than the half spent writing.

◆

After postulating that this thing might actually be successful, I started to worry about the inevitable legions of competition that would ultimately develop. Analogists surfacing everywhere, i.e., "Today on Oprah we have Bob Harrah on the show. He is one of the foremost analogists in the Delaware Valley. His name is also spelled the same forwards as backwards — thereby supporting the argument that analogists are named not born..."

This immediately threatened my "not having to work hard" theory as competition is apt to do. However, hopefully by the time the inevitable "industry shake out" comes, I will already be rich and retired.

◆

A smile is worth 2,000 words.

◆

I have a friend who called last week to update me on his life. During the day he works in "collections" and at night he works at a sporting arena as an "usher".

Apparently he got to know a season ticket holder fairly well over the course of a basketball season. As luck would have it, this guy offered to set my friend up as one-half owner in a collections business. We're talking office, phone, business connections, salary — everything. From usher to owner, just like that.

When my friend asked him, "Why me?" He said, "Well, I was your age when someone gave me a chance."

I can honestly say I hardly know anything about this guy. Regardless, I'll betcha he sleeps well at night.

◆

You gotta have a dream if you ever want it to come true.

—◆—◆—

-23-

Don't call me at all if you can't call me a friend.

◆

When my best friend hung up on me during one of my analogies (after only hearing two, mind you), I immediately felt the need to react with a vicious analogy punch. I then remembered my analogy etiquette — don't tell someone an analogy you yourself wouldn't want them to tell you.

◆

If you lower yourself to someone else's level, your children won't like the view.

◆

Cranberry juice tastes like cranberries and orange juice tastes like oranges. Wine however, is usually described with dramatic passages like, "A full and richly complex wine with a rich berry bouquet, yet delicate and elegant with a clean fragrant aroma..."

The next time my mother asks if I've "met anyone"

recently — I'm grabbing the nearest wine bottle.

"Yeah mom, I think you'd really like her. She has a dry, delicate sense of humor, is rich, full bodied..."

◆

Our families are the only ones who would wait in line in the rain to see our movie a second time.

◆

It's interesting how different sports have different standards for measuring success. In basketball, 60% success is good, and in baseball a 30% success makes you millions.

I'm not sure whether parenting is a sport — in any case, it truly is one activity where a healthy child is worth millions.

◆

If you want to save butter, butter someone up through their kids.

◆

Your loved ones and humor are very similar. Whether it's waking up from a coma and seeing your wife, or hitting a home run with your parents in the stands. Loved ones and humor will make any situation better.

◆

If you have a phone in America — you have to decide whether to get "call waiting". Now let's be honest. Shouldn't this feature be known as "call interruption"?

There is also an option "call forwarding". It forwards a call to another phone number. Someday my friend Tom will call me and it will be forwarded to my car phone. Of course, I won't be there — all my calls are being forwarded to the plane phone on flight #712. Unfortunately for Tom, by then I've already boarded a slow boat to China. There's no way I'm taking calls when I'm on a cruise — all these calls are getting forwarded to my friend, Tom. I sure hope he has "call waiting" — I'd like a tape of that conversation.

—◆—◆—

-24-

They say "you can't judge a book by its cover." I disagree. I think you can — people do it all the time. *Should* they, is the question.

I'm kinda young in years old; consequently, many people assume I don't know too much. They may be right — I'd just rather they opened the book before deciding. I usually got better grades on book reports when I read the material.

◆

paradox (par-a-doks) n. — A statement that seems to contradict itself or that doesn't contradict itself.

◆

If you prejudge people — you may end up looking at yourself in the mirror.

◆

When you argue with someone, most times you think you see things as clear as day. Chances are the other person is thinking the same thing. The question is — who's the better weatherman?

P.S. — Usually the best weatherman is the one able to change his forecast when presented with new information from the weatherman he is arguing with.

◆

Public opinion is everything — isn't it?

◆

One should make sure they have flossed their own teeth before pointing out the broccoli in someone else's.

◆

I've heard the saying, "Nobody wants your temper, so don't lose it." I've also heard that it's not too good to keep things locked up inside you. Quite honestly, I'm a little confused. In either case, I'm sure those lost tempers out there won't have a problem finding single socks.

◆

Whenever I get real dressed up — I usually wear something with a small hole in it, or a cheap watch, or...

I know sometimes it can be easy to fool other people — I just don't want to fool myself.

—◆—◆—

-25-

Horse racing is 30 minutes of time outs followed by the last play of what was a tie game.

◆

My wise brother-in-law (who trains racehorses) once said, "I don't worry about things I can't control like the weather and pole position in a horse race."

I think we could add to that list, "what racetrack bartenders put in your drink."

Who is Roger Attfield? He's the brother-in-law I referred to in the prior paragraph.

This is an inside joke — I'd explain it to you, but then it might not be an inside joke anymore — thereby resembling an outside joke more, in which case it would be exposed to the weather which, thanks to Roger, I realize I shouldn't worry about — so never mind.

◆

To horse racing: a sport where they've managed to eliminate the first two hours of a boring sporting event and just serve a two-minute highlight film where your team either loses, or comes from being behind 1-0 to win with a 2-out, 2-run homer in the bottom of the ninth inning.

◆

To Tracy and Roger (horse trainers):

You've got the ultimate baby sitting job having to clothe, feed, and shelter 50 horses without ever getting a day off. Do horses ever really grow up? Thing is, you never get any help from the horse parents or in-laws. They're always at some farm in Kentucky messing around making more horses.

—◆—◆—

-26-

Always dance while you can still hear your favorite song playing.

◆

"Some people march to the beat of a different drummer." This is okay, as long as they realize there are no bands with just a drummer.

◆

Music is the best medicine cabinet in the world.

◆

Beethoven's pharmacy has no expiration dates.

◆

Should one like classical music for the way it makes them feel; or, to rattle off symphony names and opus numbers in an attempt to impress others? Remember, music is great without the names whereas the names aren't much good without the music.

◆

"If rap music can sell, this should as well."

◆

Life is like a slow dance — it's usually more fun with a partner.

—◆—◆—

-27-

If somebody has a 100 dollar bill in their pocket and I am not able to see it, do they really have it? I don't really care unless they buy me a drink.

◆

While traveling in Costa Rica, I met a couple from Canada deciding whether to move from Vancouver to Costa Rica. We talked for awhile about the pros and cons of such a move and as they were leaving, I mentioned "at least your kids will be bilingual."

It's not for any one person to say what country is best, etc. But certainly knowing another language would assist someone in understanding the rest of the world as well as their own. There are a lot of different types of food in the world. I'd rather have several utensils when having a meal than trying to eat everything with just a fork.

◆

The saying is, "Simple minds are easily amused." Sometimes water just cracks me up.

◆

We all know people who frequently talk about their problems, etc. I understand the therapeutic benefits of discussing one's problems, but don't cross the line into dwelling on them. Learn as best you can and move on. If your hamburger comes with tomato on it, which you don't like — do you fuss and fume about it, or just take off the tomato and move on?

◆

Humbleness is like a cold beer, it makes being right or wrong just a little bit better.

Sometimes I wish people drank more cold beers. However, don't operate heavy machinery while being humble.

◆

To all the bars around the world — I thank you for leaving such a detailed credit card trail without which I would never know where I've been, let alone where I'm going.

—◆—◆—

-28-

Can you imagine a job where everyday felt like a Saturday. They're out there, don't give up just because it's still Monday in your office.

◆

I think I like this writing thing, you never have to punch in on a time card. The drawback though is it's a little tougher to punch out also. But if you love your work, there are no time cards.

◆

I remember the first time I heard the word "entrepreneur." I had gone home from college and was visiting my father for lunch. He introduced me to someone in his office and called me his "son, the entrepreneur".

Typically, I wasn't very fond of being called things I didn't know the meaning of — let alone, spell. All I was doing was importing some leather shirts from Istanbul to make some money for college. Was he referring to this, or perhaps some deeper psychological shortcoming I was not aware of?

His subsequent smile and pat on the back, however, alerted me to the positive nature of this word. Apparently, I had been an entrepreneur for quite some time — I just didn't realize it. If you take the action first — the title and its meaning will come to you later.

◆

Creativity = $(\text{what if})^2$

◆

Did you ever see a billboard that said "You could advertise on this billboard"? How effective could that space be if they need to advertise its availability? Aren't they really announcing they're not very good at their job? If they were being truthful, wouldn't the billboard really say "You can advertise here because we can't find anyone else"?

If they really wanted to get a response, they might try an ad like — "This space not available at any price." Imagine the prestige of being the ad that went on the billboard after that line.

◆

Why is it when you're a comedian, so many people want to tell you a joke, or if you're a poet they recite their favorite poem? When someone goes to a restaurant, do they bring their own food?

◆

There are two types of jobs in the world.
One where you try to fulfill your dreams —
or one where you help others fulfill their dreams.
Either job is okay — if it's your dream.

—◆—◆—

-29-

Every book starts with just one word.

◆

If anyone thinks I am making fun of them as a group or an individual — this is not true. It's the ones who don't realize it who might need to worry.

◆

Should I ever suffer a premature death for some unforeseen reason, I imagine that would somehow enhance my work. Sometimes what could have been is imagined to be better than what is. Seeking to improve my work as is one's nature — I thought I might somehow fake my death, thereby improving the quality of my writing.

To my eventual grandchildren who will someday think I have passed away — I may just be at a Braves game with Elvis waiting for my work to improve.

◆

I was thinking the other day that inevitably this book will make its way into someone's bathroom somewhere. I expected coffee tables and night stands, but I think I had been using denial when it came to bathrooms. Anyway, you've heard the saying, "If these walls could talk." — Well, I'm just glad books can't see or smell.

—◆—◆—

-30-

To costa Rican roads – They're great for inspiring writing but terrible when it comes to trying to write the inspiration down.

◆

It's amazing how third world countries have such a high population growth rate considering the popularity of cold showers there.

◆

To Chris Columbus — Thanks for stopping by.

There's an old saying that "The devil you know is better than the one you don't know." When I planned to visit Central America, some people wondered about the danger of such a trip. I thought — don't these people pay attention to the six o'clock news reporting all the fires, murders, and crimes in our country. Obviously other countries aren't perfect either, but perhaps the devil we don't know may really be an angel — we'll never know for sure until we visit their house.

◆

We are only as tall as our comrade next to us.

◆

To Costa Rica: A country with some of the world's best roads.

Before going to Costa Rica, I had been warned about how bad the roads were. Sure enough, they were nothing to brag about. As I saw more of the country, I was amazed at how much wonder there was packed in such a small place. Perhaps roads should be measured by their view instead of how many potholes they have, or how long it takes to get there from here.

◆

If you always dwell on people's faults — you yourself will never visit perfection.

◆

It's funny how certain smells, or songs, or whatever, elicit particular memories. The smell of green apple shampoo always takes me back to Brisbane, Australia as a 17 year old exchange student. What a wondrous year in every regard. To all my Australian friends who are literally standing upside down as I write this — if your nose runs and your feet smell, then you must be from down under (upside down.)

—◆—◆—

-31-

Fame is one of the world's best cosmetic surgeons.

◆

Many people are able to translate their success in one particular field like sports, into another area like acting. Genetically speaking, do they have an excellent sports gene and great acting genes, or when it comes to acting are they usually relying on another gene called "famous"?

Scientists have been studying the "famous gene" for quite some time. One group of scientists believes not everyone has the famous gene, whereas the other group believes the gene is present in everyone but can remain dormant indefinitely. Do you know which group of scientists is better known?

◆

Perfection is a museum with a long line but no inhabitants.

—◆—◆—

-32-

Every company started with just one question.

◆

Lots of things in the world need change. There are other things out there that don't.

I think the saying is — "if it ain't broke don't fix it." Thing is, sometimes people make changes to satisfy their self interest. If something is working okay, and they don't alter it somehow, it's difficult for them to take credit. Do you take a pitcher out of a game in the sixth inning if he's got a no-hitter going? Sometimes the best managers in life are the ones we never hear about.

◆

I apologize to all the customer service reps I have chewed out over the years in various industries. I know you are not the cause, but the front line of defense. As with most battles, it is the front lines that suffer all the casualties, while the generals sit on their horses at the golf club.

◆

Have you ever called the phone company and gotten a busy signal? Isn't this ironic. If you really need to talk to them, who do you call to "cut in" to tell them it's an emergency?

"Hello, is this the Cable TV company?"

"This is Nicole Korchak over on Magnolia Drive. I was wondering if you could cut the cable service over at the phone company."

"Well, I was just thinking if you turned off their cable TV, they might put their phones back on the hook."

◆

The best year I ever had included fifty-two Monday's.

◆

I have a computer I use just about everyday. I download stock charts enabling me to do technical analysis, and I'm also a member of CompuServe in case I want to know what the current weather is in Boise, Idaho.

It's funny though, when it comes to writing — my original copy is always handwritten. There's something special about discovering a letter that has your name written on it in a style (Dear Frank) you cherish and are familiar with.

Certainly I realize the future is in computer and telecommunications; however, I've promised myself my signature will always be hand-carved.

◆

Open a door for someone — it will make your passage more rewarding.

◆

"Stress" — we all get it and we all want to alleviate it one way or another. I thought about what was the essence of something that would cause stress.

Traffic has always been one of the greatest stress producers for me. We get to a red light and have to stop. I personally get really annoyed when I get stuck at the same light for two reds in a row. We all know how frustrating that can be. The essence of this stress was being somewhere and one minute later still being at that light having accomplished nothing.

Then it struck me — the irony of it all. Just what do we do to alleviate all this stress? We go on a vacation, sit on a beach, and do nothing. *The medication we take is that which caused the stress*.

Maybe for our next vacation, we should all save a bunch of money by grabbing a book and a camera, and spending five days and four nights at one of the town's nicest traffic lights.

—◆—◆—

-33-

Economists predict their forecast will probably be correct if it's not wrong.

◆

I've always been an admirer of Franklin Roosevelt. Back in the 1930's, he suggested everyone donate 10 cents towards a cure for polio. Nearly two million dollars was raised and it was this "March of Dimes" which brought about an eventual cure.

A dime doesn't go as far as it used to. I guess if we want to keep up with inflation, we need to give of ourselves even more these days.

◆

One of America's biggest deficits involves trading common sense for political partisanship.

◆

Politicians should promise not to make any promises they won't break.

◆

For every stock market or economic opinion, you can find an equally effective argument supporting the exact opposite point of view. It's not so important to be right or wrong, just make sure that when you're right — you're more right than when you're wrong.

P.S. — There is a paragraph floating around somewhere that says the exact opposite.

◆

Let's start a lobby against lobbies. What happens if this lobby is very successful?

◆

Everything has gone up in price in the last fifty years — I believe economists call this "inflation." How come old "sayings" don't seem to keep up with inflation?

"If I had a nickel for every time I've heard my husband tell that joke — I'd be rich."

Has anyone ever done the math on this? Well, I did. If he would tell that joke 10 times a day, 365 days a year, for 50 years — a total of $9,125 would be raised. I know I'll need more than that when I retire.

It seems like there must be easier ways to get rich. Maybe if we all got together and each "put in our two cents..."

◆

There is no utopia — besides, how would we pay for it?

—◆—◆—

-34-

We are all about the same height when we sleep on the ground.

◆

They say the brain has to hear something seven times before it is learned. Yes, that's right, seven times. They say the brain has to hear something seven times before it is learned. Yes, that's right, seven times. They say the brain has to hear...

Anyway, the bad news is advertising companies are apparently well aware of this.

◆

Does the body produce endorphins for prolific writers?

◆

If I were taller, I'd have longer arms and it would be easier to pat myself on the back.

◆

Many successful people have a right-hand man partially responsible for their success. I want to know where all these right-hand men are and are they all married to left-handed women?

◆

Is a black and blue thumb a sign of an errant carpenter or a colorblind gardener?

◆

Many of us take a great deal of time and effort when preparing for a night out. Eventually we are ready and outside we go.

Then suddenly, at the pinnacle of one's physical preparedness, the wind just demolishes our hair. We turn our heads, and put up our hands hoping the wind will recognize the international "I surrender" signal — it doesn't.

Your hair is the only feature with which the wind reaps such havoc. Imagine if some other feature like our nose was so easily affected.

— "Look at the nose on that guy, he must be from Chicago."

or

"You must have driven with the top down, Debbie, your nose is a mess."

— Clairol would come out with a "nose spray".

— Some guy would always be on TV talking about his "nose club for men".

— Instead of lawyers known as "ambulance chasers", we'd have cosmetic surgeons known as "tornado chasers".

— . . . .

—◆—◆—

-35-

Some think it is better to buy a drink for all their friends — I would rather have a friend for all my drinks.

◆

I recently went to a Black Tie affair in honor of some friend's engagement. Everyone went to a fair bit of expense to look virtually the same. It all seemed kind of silly to me, the women wearing black dresses and the men expressing their individuality with different bow ties.

Anyway, despite any misgivings I may have had, I ended up having a great time. I knew it wasn't because of how well everyone dressed. Usually the better dressed one gets, the less comfortable the clothing is. No, there was more to it.

And so it was to be, that in this "extreme of attire" that I came to realize how much I liked these people. Not for what they were wearing — but for how they were still able to unabashedly be themselves. Sometimes in life it takes an extreme to realize we are all equally naked under our black ties. No amount of formal attire could change my friends or make them "respectable", — perhaps that is why I respect them.

◆

Don't pick your friends based on what they can do for you — otherwise, you may find yourself the last pick.

◆

My friend Steve asked me whether "you feel guilty about not thinking about someone everyday after they've passed away?"

When you first lose someone close to you, they are in your thoughts everyday. I think Steve had reached the end of this stage and was wondering if it was okay to miss a day here and there. There is no need to feel guilty when this happens — be content in that they will live on through you. A friend will live on through a lesson on life they taught you, or a father will live on through a son's voice. You see, *imitation truly is the sincerest form of immortality*.

—◆—◆—

-36-

The "heat in the kitchen" isn't that hot once you realize it's only "room temperature".

◆

The first taste of anything is often the best, and by the end of the portion you've usually had your fill. Food has to obey this "law of diminishing returns." Otherwise, we'd all weigh 500 pounds.

◆

Your mind is a terrible thing to baste — so don't put your head in an oven.

◆

One man's brilliance is another's corn flakes.

◆

Everyone needs to work at their own pace. Walking just to and from the refrigerator is okay — if it's more than you did yesterday.

◆

People really are the same at 15 years old as 45. As they get older, they get better at changing the icing on the cake — but the flavor of the cake never really changes.

◆

Life is full of fortune cookies. Keep eating out until you find one that makes you happy.

—◆—◆—

-37-

It is better to be honest in defeat, than deceptive in the pursuit of victory.

◆

There are plenty of 6'7" people out there who aren't good basketball players. Just because someone is intelligent or shrewd doesn't necessarily mean they're great in the game of life. Everyone in the league can be a better player by working on their passing game.

◆

Negativism begets negativism and before you know it, you're the last place team that never even went from last place to next to last.

◆

You wouldn't believe the number of times I've been burned by partners. I'm probably more skeptical about some things these days, but who knows what the future will bring. In any case, I will always start every season liking my teammates and thinking we can win it all.

◆

I prefer quiet confidence — that way there aren't as many spectators in the stands if you swing and miss.

◆

To all the people in my life who have crossed my fairway and pocketed my golf ball. Thanks for the lesson — always hit your shots straight and in plain view. Good luck with your golf game, but you shan't be invited to play in my foursome.

To all those who have given me one of their golf balls when mine was lost — thank you and may our fairways cross again soon.

—◆—◆—

-38-

Isn't life about managing expectations? Here's to true love between two people — finally a case where you can let your expectations flow free without disappointment.

◆

Did you ever wonder why some people don't seem so upset at the end of a relationship? Maybe it's hard for them to feel a sense of loss for an investment they never made.

◆

A wet dream is the ultimate in "mind over matter".

◆

Have you ever spent hours working on something on the computer only to have it erased. It's a very empty feeling. Isn't this kind of what happens after putting your heart and soul into a relationship that fails?

Use computer back-up discs — it may not save a relationship, but what you have learned will help in your next one.

◆

They say married men tend to live longer than single men. Does this mean men are more sensitive than they admit, or misery loves company? Funny thing is, women live just as long married or single. Is all this so-called female emotion just a distraction whereas in the final analysis women are tougher than men?

◆

Have you ever been talking with someone when suddenly they'll throw this "big word" at you from outta nowhere?

"I was standing in line at McDonald's yesterday when this guy just perambulated (walked by) past all of..."

If you don't know the meaning of the word — you have to make that "snap" decision. Do I admit I don't know the meaning, or do I just play along hoping the definition of the word will make itself clear in the subsequent conversation?

Of course, when in doubt — I always just make fun of the word.

"Hey Mark, mind if I perambulate your date this weekend?"

◆

Too many times in life we go 50/50 on things. Perhaps if we had more relationships where both sides gave up 60% — we'd have more relationships.

◆

Everybody has their own strike zone. If we don't adapt our pitching accordingly — they'll walk.

◆

I had a good year in softball last year. There was one month when it seemed like I was making a diving catch every game. I think I enjoy fielding more because each catch is so unique whereas memorable hits are so dependent on the situation. Anyway, it was interesting — after that one month, suddenly there weren't any diving plays for awhile. Was my fielding declining? No, I don't think so. Balls hit just out of my reach weren't presenting themselves.

Maybe we expect our mates in life to always challenge us in the field. We can't always make a game-saving catch or get a game winning hit every time up. There are lots of swings and misses in between. But if we show up everyday ready to play, and love the game — we'll have a great career.

—◆—◆—

-39-

◆

People are always saying "everything in moderation". I might pay more attention to them if they didn't say this so often.

◆

Truth has one-half the syllables of fiction.

◆

"Subtle" — what a weird word. Where does the "b" go when you pronounce this word? Instead of a "silent b", is it a "subtle b". If you think someone is subtle, can they be that subtle? Do subtle people realize they're subtle? Maybe the real subtle people in the world are the ones we don't even know about.

—◆—◆—

-40-

The written word is such an exquisite snapshot of one's thoughts. I will always enjoy looking through these photographs.

◆

I recently became a "godfather". Yup — I skipped right past everyone in line to be a father and said, "Yeah, I like the father thing and all but do you have anything with some kind of deity option on it?"

"What's it called — Godfather — that's interesting. Kinda sounds like being called the supreme president of a company. How does it work?"

"...Now let me get this straight. I get this title and I don't have to mess with the day to day upkeep, but can still attend all the ceremonies?"

"Yeah, go ahead and reserve one of those for me. I'm coming straight over with cash."

◆

Your father is usually one of the few people who truly want you to achieve as much or more than they do. For as a father, that would be the ultimate vicarious elixir. To DAD w/Love — I hope to share that drink with you someday.

◆

Isn't life about doing things for other people? Now that I think about it, work is like "favor prostitution". You do your boss a favor in return for some financial consideration. The good companies are very efficient at doing favors for money. Of course, the competition is working on this same procedure. Then it comes down to which company is best at doing the customer a favor.

"Your more than welcome to use the car as often as you'd like Mrs. Walters — for a price of $20,000 dollars." (That's several favors in U.S. currency.)

Eventually the process passes from the customer to their family.

"Hey, Nancy, my little six-pack of joy. Could you pick up my dry cleaning on your way home from work?"

And ultimately the favor works its way down to one's infant offspring. A ten month old child doesn't have to do anything for anyone. They don't have to work 40 hours a week, take out the trash, put the toilet seat down, clean their room, get someone coffee, or even clean up their own mess.

Someday I hope to have a little boy. His name will probably be Harry and there will be a sign above his crib that reads: "*The Favor Stops Here*."

◆

Life is a mountain we climb so our children may see things we never dreamed of.

◆

Do you know anyone famous? If you're famous in one country, are you still famous when you go to another country where no one knows you? Just what is famous? Is it being well known? Isn't it just being liked or known by people you don't even know? Is this the important aspect in life? Isn't being respected and liked by people you know and care for the important thing?

To my family — the most famous people I've ever had my picture taken with.

◆

To my mom — she always ate in my restaurant no matter how bad the food was.

◆

I remember a particular two weeks several years ago when I ran a restaurant delivery business. These two guys staying in a hotel would order dinner from me virtually every night. They were in town for a special computer training program designed specifically for the blind. That's right, neither of them could see my ugly mug and perhaps that is why they permitted me to stay and talk.

A friendship developed and on their last night, we all went out to dinner at one of the town's nicest restaurants. It was a fantastic meal — more because of the company than anything else. Instead of dessert, we all just had a cigar. There we were, me and two blind guys grinning ear to ear and puffing on cigars. It was a sight I will not forget.

At the time I recall being momentarily saddened that

they could not see the beauty my eyes were witnessing — they were just staring off into the distance with big grins on their face.

I know now their vision was better than mine that evening. I guess sometimes you have to close your eyes if you really want to see the light, or hear the smiles.

About the Author:

Most of the time I play softball, eat out, do laundry, trade stocks, and watch television. Most of the rest of my time is spent pondering.

The most important designations I have are son, brother, and friend. I'm working towards the designation of husband and father - graduation date is still unknown.